DUSK-GLOAMING MIRRORS
AND
CASTLE-WINDING DREAMS

Other books by Hugo Walter:

THE FRAGILE EDGE

•

VELVET RHYTHMS

•

AMBER BLOSSOMS AND EVENING SHADOWS

•

GOLDEN THORNS OF LIGHT AND STERLING SILHOUETTES

•

WAITING FOR BABEL PROPHESIES OF SUNFLOWER DREAMS

•

ALONG THE MAROON-PRISMED THRESHOLD OF
BRONZE-PEALING ETERNITY

•

THE LIGHT OF THE DANCE IS THE MUSIC OF ETERNITY

Dusk-Gloaming Mirrors
and
Castle-Winding Dreams

poems by

Hugo G. Walter

Fithian Press ❦ Santa Barbara, California ❦ 1994

COPYRIGHT © 1994 BY HUGO G. WALTER
ALL RIGHTS RESERVED
PRINTED IN THE UNITED STATES OF AMERICA

PUBLISHED BY FITHIAN PRESS
POST OFFICE BOX 1525
SANTA BARBARA, CALIFORNIA, 93102

LIBRARY OF CONGRESS CATALOGING-IN-PUBLICATION DATA
  Walter, Hugo
    Dusk-gloaming mirrors and castle-winding dreams : poems / Hugo Walter.
      p.   cm.
    ISBN 1-56474-077-3
    I. Title.
PS3573.A472283D87   1994
811'.54—dc20   93-31164
                                     CIP

Contents

A Delphic-Winding Castle

A Castle by the Sea / 15
Of Dusk-Gloaming Mirrors / 16
A Delphic-Winding Castle / 17
A Millennial-Sacred Grove / 18
The Soul of the Forest / 19
Miranda-Germinating Veils / 20
The Spirit of the Palladian Bridge / 21
I Am a Gobelin-Emerald Reverie / 22
The Soul of the Mantlepiece / 23
An Ethereal-Sage Castle / 24
Traversing Bronze-Petaled Doors / 25
Corona-Saving Silences / 26
The Voices of the Clouds / 27
Pilasters of Soft-Dewed Omnipotence / 28
Of the Poppy-Breathing Chandelier / 29
A Chandelier of Maroon-Contemplating Light / 30
An Infinity of Sensibility / 31
Of Pomegranate-Sheaved Exodus / 32
The Flower of Eternity / 33
Of Amstel-Vaned Solitudes / 34
Nirvana-Gloaming Whispers / 35
The Figures in the Paintings / 36
I Am the Spirit of the Sunlight / 37
Saving the Dreams of Hermes / 38

I AM THE WHISTLER-HELIXED SILENCE

The Garden of the Lily / 41
I Gave My Heart / 42
In the Tempest-Driven Heart / 43
In Moss-Helixed Synergies / 44
Shaping Anemone-Widening Tears / 45
A Cerulean-Ancient Cerebrum / 46
A Loggia-Gentle Excrescence / 47
Amaranth-Emulating Tremors of Eternity / 48
The Kinetic-Autumn Wind / 49
I Am the Venus-Fettered Soul / 50
A Soft-Shadowed Sun / 51
A Flower on the Coffin / 52
Of Dune-Silicon Swallows / 53
In My Autumn-Germinating Loneliness / 54
Odyssey-Pale Tears / 55
Of Marble-Purple Melancholy / 56
As Emerald-Amorphous Breezes Vanish / 57
Shaping the Gothic-Liminal Heart / 58
A Thames-Spectral Abbey-Ruin / 59
I Am the Whistler-Helixed Silence / 60
The Mist People / 61
Among the Marble-Germinating Solitudes / 62
Lavender-Globed Silences / 63
Emanations of Delphic-Golden Light / 64

In the Great Chamber

    I Am the Soul of the Twilight / 67
    I Am the Rubens-Panelled Soul / 68
    When the Morning Snow Falls / 69
    In An Elysian-Petaled Cove / 70
    In Mimosa-Yellow Incantations / 71
    A Seraphic Mythology / 72
    An Amethyst-Glistening Petal / 73
    Fern-Creased Mirabelles / 74
    The Spirit of the Manse / 75
    Let the Autumn Fill Your Soul / 76
    Self-Transformation / 77
    The Apollonian-Sage Bridge / 78
    Of Glynde-Spacious Eternity / 79
    The Sunset Clouds / 80
    Of Chartres-Ogival Solitudes / 81
    In the Great Chamber / 82
    Of Amaranth-Prophetic Mirrors / 83
    Of Magenta-Vernal Hieroglyphs / 84
    Creating the Hyacinth-Streaming Twilight / 85
    I Am a Goldau-Misting Tapestry / 86
    The Ghost at Kenilworth / 87
    In Emerald-Veiled Panoplies / 88
    A Solitary Figure / 89
    I Am an Amber-Prophetic Stone / 90

DUSK-GLOAMING MIRRORS
AND
CASTLE-WINDING DREAMS

A Delphic-Winding Castle

A Castle by the Sea

There is a candelabra-gloaming castle by the sea where time
Stands still where there are no hourglass-stained rituals
Only endless-jade reflections of turquoise-coronal space
Only onyx-anemone waves of saffron-adamanthine light
Articulating seagull dreams along the Amsterdam-
   tempest shore,
There is a Tudor-luminescent castle by the sea
Where one never grows old watching the Dogana-pink frailty
Of grey-cullised time behind porcelain-silver panes
Of salmon-sheaved, Ruisdael-glowing light listening
To the aster-shivering, ancient-prophetic wind
Fill the sky with crocus-vestal, white-tympanum sails
And crescent-veiled murmurs of terra cotta galleys lost
Under the pearl-shadowed, Persephone-lambent shore,
There is a Petworth-spacious castle by the sea where silent-
Solstice, heliotrope-revealing souls live beyond grain-latticed
Pallors of molten-jagged hemispheres among
Purple-asphodel, sapphire-incarnating lilies
And pine-sceptered, conservatory-projecting gyrations
Of sun-prismed waves.

Of Dusk-Gloaming Mirrors

The Minerva-gentian light is the Elysian-pale radiance
Within the lotus-germinating soul beyond meridian-
External suns of myriad galaxies as intrinsically
Powerful as the Montacute-exalting light of the auburn-
Breathing chandelier illuminating the heliotrope-sheaved
Heart of Delphic-golden reflections only in a marble-
Pilastered, lily-converging vortex of dusk-gloaming mirrors
Is the light onyx-pure and Apollonian-soft only in a spacious-
Crenellated epiphany of sphinx-magenta auras and
   ogival-diapason
Chimes does the saffron-leavening light heal the wounds
Of mortality in lavender-asphodel, Harlaxton-winding
   silences.

A Delphic-Winding Castle

I am the fertile-cairned, Redon-chrysalis silence
At the dahlia-globed heart of the orange-cypress-pinioned,
Pomegranate-confessing tree

A Corot-white castle of cyclamen-perpetual autumns
Shears the crimson-leavened twilight from convolvulus-
Requiemed skies into the mimosa-cavernous apparitions
Of its own Cecilia-enshrining heart

Crystalline-turquoise butterflies and Hesperus-rising masks
Of pearl-helixed wisdom seal chrysanthemum-ringed souls
In jade-melodic, Cybele-deepening meoises
Of Fountains-adamanthine light

A Delphic-winding castle of red-gloaming dreams
Vanishes in the auburn-effulgent silence of its own
Perpetuity unseen by mortal eyes except when the amaranth-
Templed wind rustles golden-webbed whispers of ancient-
Hermetic horizons across Nolde-sacred vases of zinnia-
Diapason exultations

I am the Böcklin-wise, unicorn-serenading silence
Shaping heron-magenta, diva-pilastered estuary-essences
In Turner-prophetic diffusions of marble-chambered,
Mellifluous-yellow light.

A Millennial-Sacred Grove

A millenial-sacred grove where the Florentine-magenta
Confluence of the light of four porcelain-sage vases
Is the emerald-astered soul of eternity

A vase of gladiolus-conceiving, purple-iridescent muses
Receding into dove-interminable distances of pallid-
Glowing, Renoir-immaculate silences

A vase of piazza-feverish solitudes decaying into orange-
Metaphysical shells of crystalline-fertile, Fontainebleau-
Exalting light

A vase of Vermeer-listening mirrors arching into
Petrified-combing obelisks of Cassandra-elegant shadows

A vase of diachronic-lemon astral-harps animating
The sea in amphora-infinite mobiles of sphinx-hermetic,
Lunar-weeping light

A sacred-lavender grove where the diffusion of the light
Of melancholy-jade haloes of cypress-germinating,
Dusk-embalming statues is the renascence-breathing soul
Of Blickling-effulgent eternity.

The Soul of the Forest

When you walk between the two amber-majestic,
Dusk-ethereal pines at the Artemis-wreathed edge
Of the amaranth-celestial forest and tread softly,
Mellifluously on the golden-brown needles
Your soul enters forever the pristine-evolving domain
Of vernal-flaming vigils and you become forever
A part of the soul of the Ruisdael-burgeoning forest

Within the Thoth-sacred grove
A red and a white candle
On the primrose-permeating sides of a Chartres-
Breathing amaryllis-spire on a Tintern-fusing
Spectrum of silently receding mahogany-glass

Where the moon plays a cypress-vined fiddle
Of mellifluous-mazed light as the sun shapes
Emerald-scented pilasters of Rothamsted-leavening
Timelessness

Where yellow-teeming melodies of renascence-veined
Light perceive pink-rustling assonances of anemone-
Diastolic, apocalyptic-magenta dawn.

Miranda-Germinating Veils

Mandrake-burgeoning, soft-angled lichens
Spreading Bruegel-conjuring whispers of ageless beauty
Over tawny-ochre tones absorbing the oriel-curving,
Obelisk-slender light of the aurora-sophic sun

Minerva-radiating pieces of Adirondack-westerly winds
Making trees prophetic, shaping Cézanne-astral hands
In apparitional-dewed gestures of pristine-motionless
Delight pervading Phidias-vined gates of dyke-red dust
With juniper-maned contours of moat-tremulous reflections

Miranda-germinating veils of Chopin-vaulting light
Mediating between time and eternity inventing ribbon-frail
Crystals of Danube-membraned algae in kaleidoscope-domed
Masks of pandora-amicable synergies gazing at the sea
In larkspur-delicate moments of Orangerie-mutual
Transformation.

The Spirit of the Palladian Bridge

I am the spirit of the Palladian bridge
Shaping Ionic-white, cedar-fluent passions
Of amaranth-sublime, acacia-cresting light
Across obelisk-blue pallors of Dardanelles-
Rusting, hydrangea-sated memories

I am the spirit of the snow-meandering silence
Knowing that all will come to pass that is in the heart
In golden-veiled paroxysms as the Scarisbrick-frail wind
Breathes amber-gloaming eaves of damask-prismed light
Across the green-listening, sapphire-inundating sea

I am the spirit of the Hyperion-consecrating court
Spreading the Handel-wise magnanimity of my soul
Into the jonquil-fermenting sky and the diamond-
Fusing horizon I am the harbinger of coniferous-
Eclectic dreams and sunset-secluding soliloquies

I am the diadem-apocalyptic blossom of lily-expanding
Life perpetuating helicon-lambent moor-silences
In wisteria-endless arabesques of saffron-concentric
Cloud-gladioli I am the Wilton-sealing destiny
Of threshold stones wandering in diastolic-orange,
Poppy-engraving mazes of twilight-pergola,
Orphic-soaring reveries.

I Am a Gobelin-Emerald Reverie

I am the saffron-lyred heart of the Nymphenburg-lavender
Stone shaping obelisk-singing, azalea-sweeping expanses
In celestial inclinations of Apollonian groves
Carving magnolia-enlightening, ivory-exalting truths
On grail-altared, forsythia-tinted auras of Tuscan-
Illimitable urns reshaping the garland-extending vista
Of merlin-shadowed, trefoil-cresting dreams in anemone-
Weaving, silver-misting Lucerne-silences
I am the Atlantis-liminal breath of the chandelier-
Germinating epiphany investing my soul in every other
Stone, the Beningbrough-permeating, jonquil-luminous spirit
Of the Arundel-perfecting isle of Cythere-embalming
Preludes, I am a Gobelin-emerald reverie of sublime-arching,
Cypress-templed timelessness redeeming mortality
In Ispahan-veined, magenta-rising transformations
Of twilight-saving, amber-gloaming stones.

The Soul of the Mantlepiece

The Mansard-blue soul of the pomegranate-flourishing
Mantlepiece rises in marble-blossoming visions
Of diamond-lintelled solitude spreading ethereal-domed
Wisdom around the spacious-twilight chamber beyond
Triadic-virginal veils of ephemeral-mitred dust
The soul of the Montacute-timeless mantlepiece filling
The andante-tapestried room with the sunflower-lambent
Perfection of its inner illumination floating pyramid-
Extending shadows of immutable delight across my horizon-
Conceiving, Rembrandt-liminal mind shaping the eternal
Beauty of sapphire-redeeming rainbows and autumn-resined
Silences in heliotrope-gleaming, primordial-latticed
Daemons of Pythian-omnipotent innocence and hydrangea-
Ecstatic omniscience.

An Ethereal-Sage Castle

An ethereal-sage castle appears near the Orangerie-
Enclosed lake when the amber-helixed, Theocritean-
Softening twilight pours across its Belvedere-cascading
Walls and disappears in the azalea-fountained light
Of the lapis lazuli tears of diving spirits dreaming
Of Palladian bridges I saw it once in my youth
When the Sistine-cairned elms reached Parham-giant
Shadows along the edge of the azure-swelling waters
When onyx-stained breezes whispered eglantine-streaming
Harmonies in maze-fermenting lullabies when madrigal-purple
Butterflies played upon saffron-gloaming rhythms
Of Zoroastrian-seminal light there is a Gothic-liminal,
Moss-reflecting castle dividing transience from the asphodel-
Veined shadows of immortality sheltering the lemon-scrolled,
Daemon-sealing auras of eternity from ephemeral-gilded,
Sable-ewered words in the presence of the diamond-paned,
Opalescent-globed castle the questing soul reshapes itself
In dawn-perfecting calligraphies of phoenix-soaring,
Tyntesfield-effusive, emerald-calyxed light.

Traversing Bronze-Petaled Doors

Jade-enamelled, gladiolus-permeating breezes of mimosa-
Glistening, chamomile-ascending light convince time
Of its ephemeral flux though not of its mortality
At the dendrite-wizened edge of the avatar-curtained
Abyss dry-samovar mountains of cirrus-steel shadows
Shield green-petaled Pegasus-dreams of mosaic-glazed,
Ichor-promising amphora-truths from Barbizon-coronet
Whirlpools of frozen-dust, apse-angled lighthouse-gales;

In the Neuschwanstein-enshrining silence of the Gobelin-
Rustling wind I see the spiral-nurturing shadows
Of eternity lingering on auroral-refulgent, astral-
Sharing tresses of soft-blue margins of Calliope-dreaming
Meadows where alabaster-helixed clouds perpetuate
Pandora-eclectic dissonances of dormant-flickering time
Fugal-yellow threshold-voices traversing bronze-petaled
Doors of horizon-reflecting, Orion-deepening light.

Corona-Saving Silences

Flemish-orange, corona-saving silences shaping
Maroon-cypress poppy-mists into lavender-
Serenading, prism-spired lilies carving Nemi-
Fevered time on moon-tendering, jade-eclipsing
Dreams of alabaster-latent, chamomile-streaming
Obelisks, dawn-helixed, Ausonian-pallid hills
Of serpentine-gypsum, peach-inscribing light rise
Above Alhambra-laden, dune-calyxed vortices
Softening calliope-leavening tempests
Of the evening-martyred sea in marsh-emerald,
Fugal-nurturing dissonances of Stonehenge-carmine,
Albemarle-deepening light.

The Voices of the Clouds

In the Murnau-red wind the voices of the Chillon-reflecting
Clouds scatter minaret-azure dreams of sunset-diffuse graves
Across orange-tympanum horizons in amethyst-pealing,
Norham-solitary tears of laurel-veined, lemon-diastolic light

The cathedral-transmuting voices of the Fontainebleau-
    ascending
Nepheliads sing nightingale-inviolable epiphanies of ancient-
Crystalline vastness where fiery-pastel asphodels bloom
In the saffron-opulent eyes of the palomar-isled divine
In crimson-lambent cascades of Isis-lyred resonances

In the narcissi-tremulous wind I hear the Aegean-pale reveries
Of twilight-vaned cloud-poppies splaying cosmic-diaphanous
Inundations of amaryllis-cinnabar stars across Utenwarf-
    timeless
Voices of white-ripening, turquoise-deepening spaces.

Pilasters of Soft-Dewed Omnipotence

As the Scythian-majestic towers rise through the Maia-
Empyrean mists the silence of the apocalypse peals
Across the sable-merlined wind the moss-darkened clouds
Reappear and disperse in crimson-apertured cycles
Like Gunterstein-furrowing thoughts in linden-incurable
Panoplies of moor-gleaming, auburn-chasmed light
Corinthian-pinioned pilasters of soft-dewed omnipotence
Surging through amorphous-duned blizzards of white-cairned
Breezes shaping immaculate dreams of golden-veined
Pallors on lonely bridges of Palladian-wise intensity
Two figures shaping contemplative, mercurial radiances
With cypress-cascading horizons touching the sun
Through the amber-knolled haze in amethyst-enamelled
Pyres of orange-diapason light carving time
On Weltschmerz-measureless distances of Chatsworth-
    burgeoning
Streams as the diamond-lintelled meridian-tears conceive
The oracular destiny of the magenta-effusive sky
In rushing, seething billows of Geneva-equinoctial,
Fountains-whispering light the sea becomes a crystalline
Inflection breaking into a thousand angles of tempest-woven
Sighs dissolving into myriad masks of Aeolian-lyred
Shells reshaping the sun in onyx-tendrilled windmills
Of lily-gloaming, amaranth-centering light.

Of the Poppy-Breathing Chandelier

In the heart of the pomegranate-sceptered mirror
The lavender-germinating soul can see vulcanic-sage
Reflections of the poppy-breathing chandelier
In the Florentine-astered depths of the dusk-gloaming
Mirror the saffron-iridescent, Monet-crystalline soul
Can see the birth of the laurel-architraved chandelier
In sibylline-dewed atrophies of emerald-cascading light
In the Jungfrau-spherical, mistral-gesturing chasm
The marigold-listening chandelier becomes an Aeolian-vaned
Lily of madrigal-turquoise feelings spreading its Janus-
Diapason wings through grail-oracular corridors
Of the universe as the sea becomes an amber-vaulting dream
Of Eden-liminal, Meissen-labyrinthine light.

A Chandelier of Maroon-Contemplating Light

He crossed the garden of Botticelli-astral smiles
Towards the almandine-breathing light in andromeda-lithesome
Visions of Goya-petaled night shaping the sky in Fasanerie-
Laminating isles of adamanthine-sceptered liberty
Upon a baroque-gesturing urn of lavish fame where ormolu-
    gentle
Willows turn beyond the emerald-germinating horizon in sunken
Panoplies of topiary lullabies and dew-shining flames;

A trumeau-revealing chandelier of maroon-contemplating
Light in the lily-effulgent mirror of a thousand marigold-
Synthetic dreams twelve eyes of pure-onyx light luring me
Into the Florentine-mazed aura of the gilded, jade-scrolled
Frame opening the sacred-pilastered, crystalline-acanthus fold
Of eternity dissolving a diastolic-meandering soul in Blickling-
Lambent effusions of golden-mullioned gleams transforming
Intimations of the divine in auburn-gloaming aureoles
Of odyssey-helixed epiphanies in wisteria-oracular pulsations
Of porcelain-angled, Uffizi-culminating light.

An Infinity of Sensibility

There is an infinity of sensibility
In a gray-permeating, white-orisoned sky
Which the blue heavens can never offer

I am the gray-leavening spirit
Of the Aegean-vernal, oleander-rhythmed
Light suffusing galvanic-red horizons
With lichen-ochred veils of Pentelic-
Marble palms

Only the sepulchral-wise clouds
Know the nasturtia-whispering truth
About the world in amber-vaulting reveries
Of vermilion-canopied towers and autumn-
Prophetic, cross-refulgent dawns

Only the dove-brooding, rainbow-consuming
Clouds dissolve the maenad-raging, moon-
Cursed crags of mortality in Apollonian-onyx,
Willow-fermenting streams of Friedrich-altared,
Crepuscular-golden light.

Of Pomegranate-Sheaved Exodus

When the sunset-crimson cloud-haloes
Transform time into tessera-chaliced
Shadows of Brahms-prophetic light I see
The magenta-veiled towers of saffron-listening
Eternity rising from lion-winged bridges
Of purple-alabaster thalassic-poppies,
When the seagulls call dyke-vespered angels
In melisma-lintelled nebulae of pomegranate-
Sheaved exodus I see the Pythian-radiant
Towers of lavender-diastolic eternity evolving
Tarantella-wise silhouettes from iridescent-
Plasma smiles and anemone-mandarin soliloquies
Of a lonely, pensive god at the last Gilgamesh-
Architraved fold of the amber-pealing, kylix-
Fugal horizon.

The Flower of Eternity

I listen to the amphora-shaping, laurel-misting
Angels pray at the edge of the chamomile-flaming
Abyss for the Byzantine-whorled, lotus-effulgent
Flower of eternity to bloom in moor-astral breaths
Of myrrh-sated, marble-scented wind along an Atlantic-
Sceptered dune of crystal-architraved solitudes
And Sylt-vestal visionary silences, in crimson-
Webbed sunset-shadows of alluvial-kinetic waves
I see the jonquil-gazing, anemone-enshrining flower
Of eternity rising in chrysalis-lavender moons
Of saffron-petaled, Lyndhurst-spectral light.

Of Amstel-Vaned Solitudes

In the pomegranate-dewed, ethereal-gray shadow
Of the estuary-veined windmill rises a margrave-solstice
Figure endowed with Elysian-tendrilled eternity
By amber-kinetic blooms of ancient-Bavo winds and blue-
Tempest peals of Catskill-spiring willow-truths
Dispersing Promethean-tessera hymns of architectonic-
Primeval isolation, untouched by Taormina-fertile
Rivulets of vain, hourglass rituals, creating the pyramid-
Sage sublimity of sail-dissolving, saffron-tremulous
Timelessness in Hyperion-discoursing silences of cobalt-
Mediating, Amstel-vaned solitudes.

Nirvana-Gloaming Whispers

In the albatross-raptured willow-dreams
And pristine-alveolar barrow-haloes
Of the phosphorescent-yellow morning wind
I hear Pergamon-confessing coves
Of the leviathan-grailed moon,
Ganges-petaled, Rhine-plaintive murmurs
Of dusk-fragile, eternally wandering marsh-souls,
Nirvana-gloaming whispers of perpetual-sage
Reincarnations of kindred spirits, of my past souls
Reshaping the immortal edge of Debussy-veiled eternity
In lambent-arborealis transformations
Of crocus-fountained, helicon-pulsing light.

The Figures in the Paintings

There is a time of day
When all the figures in the paintings
Emerge in the spaciousness of the room
When they sit on the divan or along
The mahogany table and talk freely
As if nothing had happened
As if their willow-murmuring essences
Were as perpetual as the cyclicality of nature
When they appear from gilded frames
And chiaroscuro eternities, from Gothic-liminal
Reveries and azure-unvanquished spaces
They never change endowed by the arabesque-golden,
Acanthus-lintelled enclosure with the Blickling-
Luminescent aura of marble-germinating eternity
They never fear the vicissitudes which ravage
The flux of the world and time
Shaping the tremors of the sea along the calyx-
Mazed dream of the horizon conceiving dune-scented
Meadows in diastolic epiphanies of yellow-exalting
Light in the ethereal-primrose, amphora-echoing
Gleam of Meissen-amber silences the figures fulfill
A twilight paradise in mandrake-eloquent shadows
Where lavender-resplendent asphodels and Delphic-
Pealing, lily-gloaming reveries never fade.

I Am the Spirit of the Sunlight

I am the spirit of the hyacinth-singing sunlight
As it weaves Beauvais-sonorous fusions
Of golden-mullioned silences and jade-
Glistening horizons in heliotrope-unfinished
Distances of crimson-duned, pantheon-
Iridescent solitudes I am a Stourhead-conceiving
Reverie of jonquil-diffusing light fulfilling
The shape of the sea in the Aeolian-prophetic
Destiny of my amber-architraved, iris-evolving
Soul I am an amethyst-sacred temple of auburn-
Cascading light carving Endymion-pale inflections
Of astral-wayward immortality on Salisbury-lichened
Agoras of chrysalis-corniced squalls in magenta-
Inventing, lilac-symphonic gardens.

Saving the Dreams of Hermes

There was a traveler on the silent road
Who walked alone for miles and acacia-endless
Miles where few would dare to tread and weep
He walked away inevitably from the lichen-darkened
Vanities and orchid-masked corruptions of civilized
Illusions to the sacred forest where a lapis lazuli-
Haunted, marble-ringed castle lay upon the primeval
Heart of Nature, he strode through the laurel-
Darkening hallows of time-fettered vapors where
Only sable-ewered carrion and red-shrouded ghosts
Rise from the mistral air, they touched him not,
They let him pass as if they knew of his coming,
As if his presence were foreordained by raven-
Billowing silences, as if a spectacle of amber-
Furrowed flames illumined his inner way, the lonely
Traveler came upon the castle with the mantra-chiming,
Janus-labyrinthine door exuding pale-golden phantasma
Of philomel-mourning moor-gleams, he became a Lethe-
Sceptered resonance of diamond-effulgent light saving
The dreams of the horizon in willow-lingering chalices
Of sublime-pulsing tempests in his equinoctial-serene
Castle saving the dreams of Osiris, Athena, and Hermes
In the wreath-templed glooms and alabaster-mazed reveries
Of his Titian-effusive heart—once every thousand years
A solitary traveler knows the road to eternity
In the Salisbury-emerald profundity of his damask-
Shattered, saffron-germinating, agape-flowing soul.

I Am the Whistler-Helixed Silence

The Garden of the Lily

I wander through the mahogany-panelled, ash-creviced
Corridors of auburn-globed silences and tiara-endless
Pallors coming into the Garden of the Lily
Who welcomes me as she radiates a thousand rainbows
Of loggia-ancient, amber-gelatinous dreams into my soul
She smiles a flame of love at me and turns
Into a pomegranate eye she waves her astral-tendrilled
Reveries into my spirit and washes upon the shore
An emerald-lambent grave of galactic-pearl, Seine-dewed
Light I look into the depths of her onyx-beige eyes
And become a vale-leavening elixir of cairn-widowed,
Serpentine-mitred shadows I wade into the sea of her
Soul with marigold-pilastered intuitions of tempest-
Driven solitudes as the dusk-germinating wind echoes
Orphic-contoured sadnesses across cyclamen-confessing,
Mandala-encompassing horizons.

I Gave My Heart

I gave my nocturne-fermenting heart to the peacock-exuberant
Red of the sky where the arabesque-translucent horizon
Lingers at the copper-apertured edge of Egeskov-suspending
Evening I gave my sibyl-floating heart to the Venetian-
Webbed corolla of the sky because of its diastolic-streaming
Magnanimity beyond the mortal concerns of coal-flawed,
Clay-veined atrophies I gave my swan-consecrating heart
To the illimitable crimson-lambent, alcove-fulfilling
Souls of orange-diapason evening clouds because only they
Know of the Bernini-sceptered endlessness of the acanthus-
Furrowed, alabaster-veiled heart shaping its immortality
In Blenheim-capacious galleries of pristine-modulating light
Where agaric-grained, titan-amorphous pallors may not enter
I gave my heart to the crepuscular-red warmth of the sky
Where the soul transforms poplar-scented pain into mantra-
Soft breaths of Petworth-exalting light into ivy-trellised
Effusions of maroon-symphonic, Turner-effulgent light.

In the Tempest-Driven Heart

In the Azay-tapering shadows of the jasmine-knolled
Linden-trees I see the Ionic-fusing silences of the past
Waiting for ruby-destined galaxies to nurture them
To alpine-bowered fronds of pale-conjuring delight

In the tempest-driven heart of the primrose-streaming
Pines I hear a melisma-wild shape rise to meet muse-
Weaving visions of the heliotrope-framing sky, amber-
Veined reveries of gazebo-solemn vows germinating
Lily-deepening pools of Wynyates-madrigal light

In the Paphos-tameless whirlwinds of the chameleon-preserving
Forest I see the dark-chanting shades of minerva-ancient
Sycamores listening to Florentine-mazed amplitudes
Of dithyrambic-glistening light yearning for nocturne-
Gladiolus wings of sphinx-resolving diasporas.

In Moss-Helixed Synergies

I am the Dionysian-martyred soul of the convolvulus-shoaled
Mausoleum shaping primordial-auburn blooms of allegretto-
Paned light in Rothamsted-pulsing expanses of crystalline-
Mazed solitudes

I hear your voice as if a thousand miles beyond the edge
Of time and yet within the inner resonances, forever
Permeating the crimson-stamened, Memnon-garlanding
    echoes
Of my diastolic-veined, magenta-nomadic soul

I see the marble-gentian spirit of the Blenheim-conjuring
Tomb dissolving time in moss-helixed synergies
Of diapason-veiled, rainbow-intense stones

I see the eyes of immortal-stained time
In sapphire-haloed tears of Promethean-lyred pallors
I feel the nocturne-splintering harmonies
Of the architectonic-misting horizon in the marigold-
Arching wombs of my silver-incarnate, vernal-
Perfecting soul

I am the mantra-dappled spirit of the sunset-affirming
Cathedral knowing that there is no divine presence
Beyond the carnival-concealing walls that god is only
A marsh-chasmed figment of the grey-layered dust

I am a spherical-latticed odyssey of wisteria-
Morphine, jade-iridescent silences of a hundred mandalas
Waiting to be reborn in Florentine-wise cascades
Of grail-sceptered radiances.

Shaping Anemone-Widening Tears

I am the Aphrodite-stained water that drips from mirth-
Tranced eaves and flows into orange-diapason, cyclamen-
Virulent streams of chrysanthemum-furrowed, Knowlton-
   vaporous reveries
I am the Shalott-lambent water that shapes stone-
Haunting veils of chamomile-sceptered truth in Munch-
Tremulous memories of our pristine-refulgent love
I am the Florentine-pealing water that made our lives
A damask-crimson unity and carved your life in the astral-
Labyrinthine resonances of my iris-magnanimous,
   Aeolian-entranced soul
I am the sibylline-pallid fountain of despair
That soars longingly towards the Lindisfarne-
Darkening sky on dove-whispering scythes of wayward,
   moss-bridled moons
I am the laurel-altared cascade of silent-liminal hope
Shaping anemone-widening tears in crystalline-veined
Pools of Michelangelo-gloaming, ring-vaulting twilight.

A Cerulean-Ancient Cerebrum

I am the moss-primeval northside of a cemetery-apsed
Wall where only Brancusi-corniced dreams and kinetic-
Soaring reveries appear to appease the onyx-marrowed streams
Of iris-silent tears flowing from primordial-sepulchered eaves
Of my Merevale-gloaming heart where no one ever comes
Except the translucent-crippled soul to feed the heath-
Whispering swallows and the lavender-transomed ferns

I am a cerulean-ancient cerebrum of sycamore-bearing,
Zodiac-encompassing stones listening to the solitary-
Opulent zephyrs of amber-helixed, agate-chastening time
I am the fir-arching embodiment of Samothrace-liminal
Sadness hearing the glib, spangled words of the people
Going to church and knowing there is no god anywhere
Except the spherical-webbed soliloquies of dusk-gloaming,
Dawn-twittering mirrors.

A Loggia-Gentle Excrescence

The horizon is a Beauvale-iris reminiscence of opalescent-
Angled light though it cannot permeate the cupola-helixed,
Atelier-sonorous canons of unearthly, cubist-raptured pallors

Madrigal-singular pieces of anemone-widening souls drip
Mellifluously from the Venetian-mauve tapestry in Chambord-
Gusting chords of emerald-evolving light

Marble-reflecting aureoles and estuary-jade marquesas
Convene orchid-candled vales of Tyntesfield-ascending graves
The horizon is a loggia-gentle excrescence of vellum-arching
Light though it cannot vanquish the thorn-rhythmed gates
Of rose-splashing, Dedham-veiled torment.

Amaranth-Emulating Tremors of Eternity

The only god is within us
Alone, furtive, mysterious
In its elfin-frail autonomy
Completing the self in amaryllis-veined
Harps of autumn-suffusing light
I listen to the silence of the snow
Speaking of divine-subterranean, emerald-
Vaulting shadows more lovely than
The ripening of Moselle-refulgent vines
I see endless footsteps in onyx-white stillness
Streaming in azalea-sentient circles towards
The Wartburg-pinioned, hibiscus-radiant center
Of the earth perpetuating the cedar-swelling
Exile of twilight tombs I feel the seraphic-
Laminating tranquillity of glacial-apsed
Wastelands of Caspian-shattered waves
I shape amaranth-emulating, Beethoven-iridescent
Tremors of eternity in honeysuckle-pulsing
Ravines of hermetic-moist, sage-encompassing
Dreams.

The Kinetic-Autumn Wind

At the dyke-fluttering edge of the ark-poised horizon
The Windsor-gloaming aureole-vortex is the final
Gaze of the agape-shattered divine in arborealis-
Pulsing, myrtle-congealing waves of aster-soaring
Light, Goldau-listening seagulls wandering in a tympanum-
Softening pastiche of phosphorescent-granite lulls
Miles from ocean havens Archimedean-veiled swallows
Floating across juniper-duned silences in the end
Only the kinetic-autumn wind conceives sea-fevered,
Hibiscus-shaping dreams of Atlantis-converging silences.

I Am the Venus-Fettered Soul

I am the Venus-fettered soul of Hever Castle
Wandering through mahogany-eternal silences
Of the banqueting hall and timber-framed courtyard
The hemlock-shadowed gallery and dust-lacquered library
In Jacobean-rising breaths of ancient-panelled,
Fern-congealing light I wander through the poppy-fragrant
Melancholy of Anne Boleyn's oratory and Anne of Cleve's
   chamber
As I shape my soul in renascence-pallid tremors of Elizabeth
And jade-hollied fountains of heraldic, agitated blood-dreams
I can never cross the moat escaping forever in inner
Courtyard-oases of apocalyptic-lemon light saving
And redeeming the cyclamen-escutcheoned spirit of the manor
In my damask-veined soul perpetuating autumn-flamed
Profusions of pearl-torrential distances across Parian-sunken
Eons of opalescent-vestal, dirge-sceptered amplitudes;

O fountain of divine-golden light
Heal my thrice-battered soul, shape my Shalott-bronzed
Soul anew in cerulean-widening pools of damask-pink light
Transform my pain to Hyperion-tendrilled rivulets
Of sapphic-holy, marigold-effulgent love.

A Soft-Shadowed Sun

A soft-shadowed sun sheared from the evening-
Latticed sky by sulphur-grey-rising strokes
Of calico-masked resin as the Cisalpine wind
Remembers Sistine-auguring visions of zinnia-
Expecting, Renaissance-mazed frescoes
Chastening velvet-minstrel filaments of time
In pristine-orchid vases as stray pilgrims
Carve a Gethsemane-moist path through perpetual
Veils of mendacity to the green-sage, Lethe-sealing heart
Of immortal twilight where purple-jonquil
Calyx-vigils convene chrysalis-floating, bronze-longing
Fountains and delta-conceiving pyramid-intuitions.

A Flower on the Coffin

He stayed beside the coffin for hours
And days when she died feeling that death
Had struck him too and wondering at its strangeness
For never again as a mortal would he talk with her
Or look into her eyes knowing that they mirrored
His love, never again in all the eons and centuries
Of the world would he be with her except in spirit
And he wondered how a benevolent god could allow this
A stream of flowers bore the coffin to its final home
Where only haggard stones and dusty-windswept leaves
Remind of a brief interval of life and then vanish too
As he kneeled upon the ground beside her grave prostrate
In grief and adoring anguish a vision rose upon his
Inner eye that there was no god at all a vision
As radiant and irreversible as the light of the conversion
Of St. Paul on the road to Damascus, and yet perhaps
There is a fragile-mitred heaven where dead souls wander
In labyrinthine contentment or astral-misting delight,
When the evening wind rushed across cemetery solitudes
In amber-veiled matrices of Botticelli-lambent light
He became one of the primrose-carving reveries
On the coffin and forever a phoenix-lonely,
Heliotrope-wandering soul.

OF DUNE-SILICON SWALLOWS

When the sea glistens
In the morning tide
I hear the gulls calling
Anemone-ripening waves in ancient-
Alabaster incarnations of Etruscan-lambent wisdom,
When the aureole-fermenting spray
Shimmers in the morning sun
I hear your voice in calliope-
Lost caverns of dune-silicon swallows,
When the sea glistens
I hear the crystalline-pale murmurs
Of our love washing upon the evening
Shore in carmine-crenellated rivulets
Of sable-astered time,
When the sunset-drenched spray
Thunders across Gemini-moist sands
I hear the gulls scatter time
In anodyne-tempest lagoons
Of cathedral-veined, Corinthian-soft silences.

In My Autumn-Germinating Loneliness

In my autumn-germinating loneliness
I take upon myself the mandrake-tremulous
Loneliness of the world I am the amber-winding,
Willow-circling bridge of sighs where broken,
Desolate hearts mourn the irrevocable passing
Of their lives so full of lilac-nurturing love
And forsythia-veined generosity of soul scorned,
Misunderstood by voiceless ghosts and exiled lullabies

In the middle of the bridge two giant columns
Stretch deep into the water containing the tombs
Of two lovers, separated in death as life,
The epitome of dahlia-eclectic hearts
Except on equinoctial days when the auburn-helixed
Twilight caresses the stone in emerald-lyred curves
Their crocus-expanding souls arise and meet in diamond-
Panelled reflections of orchid-sowing tears

And when the jade-rapturing mist clears in daffodil-
Perfecting silences of Elvetham-diaspora harmonies
I see a saffron-effulgent synergy of almandine-hermetic
Light shaping the soul of the bridge in sphinx-fragile
Intimations of the vermilion-gloaming horizon
In damask-opulent tendrils of Thames-primordial,
Nasturtia-infinite solitudes.

Odyssey-Pale Tears

A Hermes-lonely, logos-inviolable wanderer staring
Across the Atlantic-crepuscular cove in an indigo-
Cascading cloud of jonquil-sacramental reveries
Watching for the ambrosia-chanting ocean
To divide in a maroon-tempest zodiac of seagull-almandine
Echoes shaping ibis-cracked graves in purple-alabaster
Cylinders of crescent-sabbath light soaring ancient-kylix
Whispers of cemetery-mandolin dreams across pale-swollen,
Grain-jaundiced headstones along the Gemini-vaulting,
Amen-raising horizon;

Odyssey-pale tears roll down his face
In cumulus-casting breaths of emerald-sated
Sculptures spilling time from Arcturus-fevered
Dreams onto the syrinx-wounded shore
Tears streaming dove-gelatinous tenderness
And sapphire-tympanum exodus across magi-
Vaulting harmonies of Arcadian-releasing,
Oleander-tolling rhythms tears swelling cinnabar-
Uranium spheres of megalithic, unfinished, crocus-
Mirroring light across dahlia-vascular, mimosa-
Pealing gardens of pine-radiant, soft-eternal hearts.

Of Marble-Purple Melancholy

I am the albemarle-deepening stream of marble-purple
Friedrich-liminal melancholy purifying the soul
Of the Jacobean-desolate hall taking the galactic-frail
Sadness of the manorial-gabled aura of renascence-silent,
Apocalyptic-wise paintings and Pythian-white, almandine-
Embering statues into my diastolic-vaned, sunset-refulgent
Soul for no god cares for such hallowed spaces but the saffron-
Nomadic spirits of the great chambers weaving delphinium-
Soaring melodies of poppy-breathing light in the Shadwell-
Conceiving hearts of ancient-prophetic stones

I am the gavotte-primordial, prelude-perfecting silences
Of the calico-transomed clouds as they hover gently over
Rosette-ivory balustrades rising into the lotus-enchanting
Sky beyond brown-cairned branches I am the silver-dappled
Melancholy of the elliptical-gusting morning sky still
Suffused with Fountains-tremulous thoughts of myriad-seeding
Snowflakes and legato-pallid amplitudes I am the majestic-
Valed grayness of the jade-escutcheoned heavens carving
Ochre-masked epitaphs of crystalline-apsed leaves on alpine-
Baroque, Promethean-lyred solitudes.

As Emerald-Amorphous Breezes Vanish

Only a convolvulus-astered ruin traced by Ionic-
Fading furrows where once the abbot's house stood
Now moss-distending stone burgeons in peach-dappled,
Melisma-fraying lights as emerald-amorphous breezes
Vanish into Elizabethan-soft peals and Gothic-ravined
Echoes of Penshurst-lost dominions, Langenburg-fusing
Souls languishing at the sable-cairned edge of eternity
As moly-elliptical abysses cluster in sibyl-divergent perfection
A jade-misting reminder of the past, a marble-pallid
Reflection that everything animate, even Tiber-meandering
Stones, passes away in the Foscari-willowed corridors
Of dune-rusting mortality—only fragile memories
Of Einsiedeln elegance linger in the omega-shrined visions
Of the Corinthian-vaulting spirit of the Valle Crucis-
Sceptered ruin for time never separates kindred souls
And their Promethean-blossoming, diastolic-orange dreams.

Shaping the Gothic-Liminal Heart

I am a red-deepening, ark-translucent spiral
Of apocalyptic-white, Upton-vaned light
Shaping the amber-streaming, Gothic-liminal heart
Of the deluge-undulating universe in gladiolus-
Veined tones of meridian-nurturing, cherry-misting
Helixes and almandine-oval scars of serpentine-
Angled light I am the genesis-lavender,
Lily-enchanting wind redeeming astral-escutcheoned
Contours of diamond-expanding glades and magnolia-
Sentient, arabesque-metamorphosing graves
In architectonic-crystalline shadows permeating
The sun with the yellow-opalescent fragility
Of mortal-lacquered, primrose-gelatinous tears
I am an Aeolian-architraved whirlpool of primordial-
Crimson, andante-murmuring blossoms falling
In cairn-dewed, untamed dissonances on the wisteria-
Laced, mezzotint-paned abyss of blue-collapsing,
Candle-stoned spring.

A Thames-Spectral Abbey-Ruin

There is a Thames-spectral abbey-ruin bleeding
Apse-scented tremors of Kedleston-azure eternity
Through broken-pyred, zephyr-confessing stones
And alabaster-filigreed harp-murmurs,
A kobold-smouldering reverie of Melpomene-
Eglantine light carving the dove-abiding
Margin of lavender-architraved genesis
On Elysian-pulsing rainbows of marble-dissolving
Cloud-haloes, an estuary-gusting, emerald-streaming
Staircase behind calico-breathing crypt-reflections
Leading through Stygian-laminating gates and shadow-
Exiled paths ascending asphodel-burgeoning, rainbow-
Diffusing valleys and cinnabar-vaulting, Wessex-
Stamened silences.

I Am the Whistler-Helixed Silence

I am the soul of one apart from life absolved
From the agitations of evanescence by a melancholy-
Profound yearning for diamond-liminal absolutes,
Distanced from mortality in the crystalline-tangible
Abyss of Versailles-fragile, alpine-gesturing creations

I am the Whistler-helixed silence of the cathedral-
Nocturne sea waiting for dusk-jade elixirs of saffron-
Frescoed light to save rainbow-corniced vigils
From mesa-jagged epitaphs of broken-piered dreams

I am the Ruisdael-gentian intuition of the Eldena-
Lavender leaves crossing Sevres-enchanting apertures
Of serpentine-crannied lagoons in damask-veiled memories
Of apocalypse-perpetuating, oriel-carving solitudes

I am the velvet-eaved silence of the Great Chamber
Where only Elizabethan-panelled shadows linger
In diastolic-mullioned panes of Corinthian-marble,
Sapphire-cascading mantlepieces

I am the emerald-veined pallor of a collage-mantled
Diaspora of white-rose petals permeating pink-leavening
Stones in lily-soaring reflections of Palladian-apsed
Dreams I am the Friedrich-capacious silence of porcelain-
Valed souls conceiving eternity in strawberry-virulent
Seclusions of windmill-fermenting, arabesque-silvering light.

The Mist People

In a tetrahedral-mazed river of grey-knelled
Fog the mist people rise to watch the sky
Vanish in a purple-cymbal haze of mandrake-
Androgynous winds

Towns and villages masked and moved by crocus-
Alabaster splashes of sulphurous-circled light
Into another dimension of time
Where the mist people reign on auburn-marble,

Nemi-apocalyptic thrones of delta-winged clouds
As the silver-layering sea washes time away
Into a Balleroy-frescoed lagoon of hibiscus-
Jettied, calypso-leavening dreams;

The mist people shaping a new blue flower
Of Delphic-gloaming, saffron-pealing light
In the leviathan-veined, mobile-swirling atrium
Of the philomel-sacred, mimosa-reflecting glade

When diamond-pulsing eyes of almandine-shelled
Light conceive archipelago-crimson veils
Of Merevale-evolving, narcissus-fragile dusks.

Among the Marble-Germinating Solitudes

Among the marble-germinating solitudes of ancient-tapestried,
Tympanum-veiled halls I wander through auburn-diaphanous,
Chatsworth-liminal globes of pearl-swelling tears
I bear oceans of sadness in my spacious-pink, Rhine-vaned soul
When the evening-tremulous gleams of maroon-chastening
    sunsets
Warm the Blenheim-exalting stones I arise and recast my soul
In the stucco-apsed, Ionic-converging auras of the chiaroscuro-
Fluent, organ-resonant picture-gallery I am the twilight silence
Saving the monumentality of the house in my dawn-effulgent
    soul
A grail-sacred space of cairn-pervasive emptiness where cries
Of delight, despair, and darkness are heard no more I am a cypress-
Lonely spirit filling the desolate-sighing corridors with
The gentle abandon of the saffron-helixed, Meissen-crystalline
Twilight.

Lavender-Globed Silences

I am the amethyst-sealing silence of the Hesperus-
Cadenced divine-hiatus shaping the darkness in gladiolus-
Scented rivulets of amaranth-soaring, diamond-immaculate light
I am a twilight-canticled fountain of Aphrodite-seething
Shadows pervading time in apocalypse-ringed apertures
Of loggia-embering, hieratic-astered tapestries
I am the crimson-architraved tranquillity of harp-glistening,
Orphic-refulgent Parnassus;

Lavender-globed silences perusing the exodus of time
In Fontainebleau-sated echoes of sunset-swelling cloud-helixes,
Turquoise-pleated poplars sealing deluge-conceiving horizons
In carmine-trellised chimes of Venetian-scattered limestone-
Coronas as miranda-languishing mirrors of red-molten staves
Break into plasma-endless myriads of Iliad-tempest reflections
Of platinum-soaring, crocus-masking truths.

Emanations of Delphic-Golden Light

I come out of the sable-threshing silences of gargoyle-
Screaming night into the gladiolus-urned, rose-sceptered
Garden reshaping the sun in maroon-adamanthine vortices
Of crystalline-tendrilled, Eden-liminal light
Transforming the stars into Mansard-eglantine hearts
Of saffron-wandering profundity

I peruse the auburn-spacious eyes of loggia-centering
Twilight in pale-azure gyrations of pyramid-breathing,
Ausonian-graceful dreams journeying through Apennine-
Gossamer tears of amaranth-sacred, muse-unvanquished
Solitude

I follow the Pegasus-cascading seed of Aegean-contemplating
Wails across carnelian-androgynous sands of calyx-angled
Hourglasses I fulminate an arborealis-converging tempest
Of vulcanic-apertured light in mandrake-dispersing
Corridors of Caspian-redemptive, Euganean-embering time

I weave emanations of Delphic-golden, melisma-jade light
Into hermetic-astered recesses and amethyst-canticled
Divinations of orphic-mazed reveries as the andante-
Streaming, willow-leavening wind heals the Parham-lambent
Garden in a Lethe-resonant paroxysm of autumn-crepuscular,
Windermere-lustred fury.

I͟n͟ t͟h͟e͟ G͟r͟e͟a͟t͟ C͟h͟a͟m͟b͟e͟r͟

I Am the Soul of the Twilight

I am the Sebastian-embering soul of the wisteria-
Rustling twilight sealing mortality in crystalline-
Pinioned globes of Isis-soaring, Merevale-vascular light
I am the honeysuckle-pallid soul of the zodiac-evolving
Twilight shaping broken hearts in alabaster-red-arpeggios
Of salmon-androgynous, pollen-procreating silences

I am the primrose-diffusing soul of the Zarathustra-
Cadenced evening wandering through margrave-desolate,
Alabaster-panelled halls echoing the cosmic despair
Of jasmine-endless, frieze-perpetuating solitudes
In the silver-marrowed depths of my orchid-stained,
Nepenthe-melodious soul I transform Atlas-seething,
Dune-permeating silences of vesper-astered, hexagonal-
Misting galleries abandoned by mortal touch into self-
Germinating suns of rhapsodic-liminal, Cyclades-effusive
Light.

I Am the Rubens-Panelled Soul

In the azalea-vaulted corridors of the east cloister
Linger marble-veined memories of ancient-madrigal silences
A Tudor-domed mantlepiece of rainbow-persisting arabesques
Exudes hyacinth-parabled, Vishnu-apsed voices
Of oaken-pilastered, Gemini-lyred dreams
Rose-trellised crosses perceive the seraphic-misting flux
Of the sable-cairned dance in Vesuvius-rustling flames
Of mandrake-dewed, golden-diaphanous elixirs
I am the Rubens-panelled, porcelain-blossoming soul
Of the zephyr-carving, astral-dawning gallery
Restoring the vermilion-architraved, obelia-murmuring
Euphonies of the gargantuan-chasmed manorial halls
In ruby-decaying excrescences of Godington-jonquil light
In auburn-elusive incarnations of Blenheim-ethereal,
Fugal-pristine mirrors.

When the Morning Snow Falls

When the morning snow falls in agate-soft whispers
Of chiaroscuro-embering light a painting emerges
On the eastern-fluted edge of the solitary-gazing elm
Within the golden-sceptered frame is a vision
Of a primrose-conceiving, gladiolus-arbored paradise
Of pastoral-eglantine silences, a painting of Giverny-
Refulgent light suspending the gargantuan-lambent spirit
Of this diaspora-veined paragon of ancient-flowering
Wisdom reshaping mortal-laminating rays in immortal-jade,
Self-perpetuating beams of saffron-gloaming light
Reminding nature of its immanent renaissance
In almandine-effulgent synergies of sunset-deepening
Melodies as suddenly as it arose from Geneva-whorled
Vapors the painting vanishes in lily-chasmed memories
Of damask-architraved solitudes sealing time in Norham-
Cadenced estuaries of Euganean-liminal delight.

In An Elysian-Petaled Cove

In an Elysian-petaled cove at the purple-sabbath edge
Of the titanic-foaming falls there is a Chamonix-hallowed
    village
Of Flensburg-lucid permanences and butterfly-mimosa
Cupolas where time, as night, passes away in the Sistine-
Chastening radiance of philomel-auroral prophesies

A symphonic-astral oasis of Poseidon-nurtured
Silences and mercureal-jade ecstasies
Of russet-trembling, dew-glazed light
Beyond rose-engraving serpentine-mountains
And sirocco-cresting leviathan-plains

A gladiolus-converging sacristy of sapphire-
Etching dreams and Andes-aureole visions
Nestled in poppy-cloistered, turquoise-mantra
Pools of Corot-effulgent, Aeolian-lyred
Twilight

Where the inviolable-glowing shadows of evening
Cascade through peacock-discerning, narcissus-
Conceiving layers of Versailles-rippling,
Gargantuan-auburn mirrors into marble-architraved
Dawns of crimson-hermetic synchronies
And chrysanthemum-radiating, virgin-pealing solitudes.

In Mimosa-Yellow Incantations

As the mist clears I see apocalyptic-white angels
   playing the Chillon-auguring ritual of timelessness
   in Dogana-yellow globes of lily-breathing,
     astral-latticed light

As the mist clears I see twilight-amber
   temple-pallors falling upon the castle ruins
   engraved in myrrh-evening, azalea-diaphanous
     silences

As the mist clears I see the hyacinth-golden light
   emanating from the eye of the divine shaping
   sacred-alluvial tremors of eternity reunifying
     amethyst-sealing wisdoms of ancient-textured
     horizons with cypress-wandering islands

Of Jungfrau-suspending gladiolus-truths, when the mist
   clears I see marigold-seraphic butterflies dissolving
   time in mimosa-lavender incantations of diamond-ethereal,
     autumn-helixed light.

A Seraphic Mythology

When the autumn wind ripens aquamarine-lexis
Cemetery-souls watching over ancient-groved
Wartburg-chimes and Andromeda-sealing, Pindar-gentian
Moon-graces apocalypse-crested angels dream reflectively
In animate-minds and Promethean-souls of immortal-sheaved
Cyclical-phases of grail-sceptered reincarnations,

When the acanthus-yellow sunset-wind permeates
Lambent-megalith, genesis-turbulent horizons the olive-
Trellised chateau of Auvers and the amaranth-mandarin
Karakal-cloister disperse zinnia-sonorous
Hosts of angels into the empyrean-diastolic dominion
Of cerulean-modulating heavens,

Angels crossing between contiguous dimensions of time
From the realm of acropolis-veined, pyramid-iridescent
Spirits to the snowdrop-wreathed domain of magi-releasing
Shepherd-aureoles perfecting souls for the immanence
Of autumn-gloaming, sunflower-exalting eternity

Angels guiding and refining swan-chancelled
Soul-energies of fleeting, motionless mortals
In Elysian-wandering spaces of crocus-integral auras

Angels creating crescent-projecting effusions
Of orange-apteryx light along the heron-witnessing,
Concentric-perpetual threshold of carmine-blue,
Stained-glass infinities

Angels revitalizing nabi-serene myriads
Of solstice-souls shaping crystalline-violet
Reincarnations of ruby-cairned, hyacinth-candled dreams
In oasis-striated vales of amber-timeless, anemone-rhythmed
Silences

An Amethyst-Glistening Petal

The gray-whispering, amber-veined clouds have a profound
Wisdom said the northern wind far beyond that of the
   pallid-blue heavens
A wisdom of sibyl-converging stones preserving heliotrope-
Mazed visions of damask-silvering eternity

The majestic-blue, topaz-radiant clouds have a supreme
Wisdom said the southern wind far beyond that of the
   alabaster-gray endlessness
A wisdom of sea-inventing, turquoise-architraved
Echoes of cedar-permeating eternity

Only the amaranth-crystalline light of the Pythian-listening,
Carnation-weaving evening knows the truth as it shapes
Sunset-tympani in Nolde-gloaming helixes of candelabra-
   magenta melodies;

The clouds smiled upon me in their marble-effulgent,
Pastel-galactic magnanimity lifting my soul
Into their hibiscus-expanding, lapis lazuli-conceiving
Mists where I saw the mandrake-confessing, iris-brooding
Gardens of eternity illuminating the Harlaxton-towering
Dome of heaven, in the emerald-singing, chrysanthemum-
Glowing silences I heard asphodel-pulsing reveries
Of lily-germinating, Turner-iridescent light
I became an amethyst-glistening petal of the Hesperus-
Eloquent cloud-heart floating on Isis-cascading
Intuitions of Aegean-discovering, Atlantis-divining light.

Fern-Creased Mirabelles

Fern-creased mirabelles of daffodil-pilastered light
Suffusing sibylline-vaulting hieroglyphs of Giverny-
Lavender timelessness at the Ganges-lily heart
Of hydrangea-procreating ponds of purple-lacquered,
Golden-radiating light, lemon-zodiac blooms
Germinating ancient-furrowed calligraphies of anemone-
Mirroring light in astral-labyrinthine omens
Of crystalline-pollinating, dusk-orange temple-orchids.

The Spirit of the Manse

In the amethyst-streaming, Wynyates-enclosing mist
Of jonquil-maned, almandine-equinoctial silences
I see the spirit of the manse rise above the myriad-
Astering roofs and pink-variegated turrets becoming
A sacred space of jasmine-rolling hills and amaranth-
Dewed lawns where maple, oak, and pine blossom daily
In pristine-exalting fountains of orange-diapason,
Camellia-architraved light I am the silver-leafed,
Stourhead-wise spirit of the manse shaping broken hearts
Of crimson-languid melancholy into flamingo-shadowed trees
Of Gemini-sceptered light I am the emerald-conjuring
Spirit of amber-timeless valences suffusing the gate
Of ancient-heraldic signs with my Venetian-exiled,
Hibiscus-latticed dreams reshaping lonely hearts in damask-
Haloed crocuses of wild-empyrean innocence

Along the hyacinth-breathing edge of the Palatine-misting
River is a grail-conceiving castle where the heliotrope-
Exalting silence of the Delphic-golden light redeems
The longevity of time where maroon-asphodel silences
Recreate the Schönborn-perpetual pallor of willow-vaned love.

Let the Autumn Fill Your Soul

Let the autumn fill your soul with Elysian-cosmic
Sadness with the hydrangea-fluted melancholy
Of piazza-apparitional evanescence as impetuous, red
Leaves glisten through your hands for only the soul
Embalmed in Dogana-wise sadness can prophesy
His own imminent, unvanquished eternity
In Zoroastrian silences of magenta-crystalline light
Let the sea fill your crocus-raptured soul
With astral-mazed chasms of sapphire-tameless,
Giorgione-melodious light
The Belton-twilight wind shapes the darkness
In odyssey-silver chimes of daemon-ethereal loveliness
As the sea seals time in Florentine-pale eyes
Of lapis lazuli-wandering sculptures of amber-
Vaulting, hyacinth-echoing light.

Self-Transformation

I waited by the sea for the apparition
To emerge from heliotrope-magenta waves
I waited to behold the golden-dewed chalice
In his turquoise-ewered hands
And as he came upon the shore
The waves drove tempestuous-lintelled cries
Across the sands towards emerald-sated skies
And as he held the Hever-vestal chalice
Over the Aeolian-moist reveries an auburn-
Tendrilled sunset-gleam arose from indigo-
Spectral clouds to pierce the shining vortex
And as they touched the old world ceased to be
A deluge of crimson-mantled, cedar-haloed light
Vanquished the semblance of a world and created
A new arabesque-conceiving tapestry of life
The apparition became the new sun and I became
The sea along the amaranth-templed shore where
Penshurst-arching silences share onyx-scrolled
Divinations of sacred time with melancholy-
Raptured sighs of seagull-wandering, iris-yearning
Solitudes and the chalice became the mantra-pulsing
Horizon where sibylline-veiled eternity meets
The Arcadian-possessing pause of Pleaides-curving
Infinity.

The Apollonian-Sage Bridge

I am the voice of the Mozart-soaring light
Shaping chamomile-leavening blossoms
Into almandine-eclectic suns of Michelangelo-gloaming eternity

I am the silence of the Grieg-misting darkness
Shaping cairn-willowed eaves of tiara-masked
Radiances into Böcklin-mitred isles of Hades-astered moons

I am the veil of the Picasso-horizoned morning
Transforming crimson-globed spaces of lavender-
Vestal light into Isis-effulgent melodies
Of poppy-weaving, amber-helixed dreams

I am the jonquil-ringed, Apollonian-sage bridge
Of Rhadamanthus-echoing, emerald-pilastered
Twilight connecting life and death in pink-
Ethereal, Elysian-tendrilled seas of Beethoven-
Luminescent, lily-diapason cherry-blossoms.

Of Glynde-Spacious Eternity

I listen to the dusk-pealing amaryllis-lambent silences
Of ancient-lacquered shadows meandering
Through jade-apsed clearings of Camelot-enthroned
Wilderness as the hourglass-congealing breeze
Radiates violet-weaving whispers in heliotrope-
Softened crannies of agaric-widening tombs

I am the white-cairned, lotus-astered perpetuity
Of stone-martyred silences suspending gray-stained
Dooms of Venus-thorned light in lavender-oracular
Cupolas of Delphic-crystalline, Eroica-unvanquished
Reveries;

I feel the cypress-consoling silences of the Barlach-
Reciting stones in my hands lichen-dreaming etudes
Growing into my hands nepenthe-pallid euphonies
Filling my hands with andante-coronal pulsations
Of onyx-inner, alcaic-saving wisdom

I feel the Rodin-elegiac stones sharing pantheon-
Moist whispers of Glynde-spacious eternity
With auburn-resined bands of mourning-dappled
Flesh shaping my hands in dusk-glistening
Intimations of crescent-apertured, gold-enflaming
Light.

The Sunset Clouds

The sunset clouds are soft-decaying, chamomile-
Straying angels of palomar-isled, Pissarro-eaved light
Magenta-pealing mournings of serpentine-angled,
Levitan-astered light amaryllis-pulsing, Dogana-
Sentient echoes of marsh-templed, lotus-harped light
Shaping the Amazon-undulating, Elbe-celebrating flame
Of gargantuan-persevering life in the space
Of a few lilac-chasmed, porcelain-helixed moments
Suspending time long enough for primordial-cinnabar
Cloud-souls to enter the Maggiore-veined,
Uffizi-valed prism of bronze-pealing eternity.

Of Chartres-Ogival Solitudes

I listen to the chrysalis-ranging, purple-oracular
Leaves speaking of Chartres-ogival, marble-sentient
Solitudes at the Lethe-gendered edge of the crimson-
Angular, iris-deepening abyss

I listen to the white-mullioned tremors of the alpine-
Inviolable sky shape the lily-winding ease of pyramidal-
Vermilion intuitions of hermetic-golden, Murillo-
Soaring light

I listen to the Couperin-fragrant leaves revealing
The orphic-magenta soul of the crystalline-sage,
Bamboo-ravined horizon in salmon-cresting soliloquies
Of jasmine-ethereal, Isis-enchanting convolvulus-shades

I carve cathedral-veined, troika-misting silhouettes
Of twilight-masking eyes on mantra-effusive etudes
Of ancient-vernal seas as the amaranth-leavening wind
Seals andante-effervescent aureoles of ivy-latticed,
Jade-sceptered light in Shadwell-rising, diaspora-
Vaulting courtyards.

In the Great Chamber

In the Great Chamber
You don't have to worry about headstones,
Graveyards, or eulogies you can spread
Your soul out on the turquoise-paned marble
As if you were entering a Montacute-crystalline frieze
In the Great Chamber
You can congeal time in amber-angled vapors
Of onyx-mullioned light where the sea is a sibyl-
Wounded reverie of amaranth-templed silences
Shaping autumn-winged intuitions of eternity
On diaspora-helixed solitudes of sphinx-resolving vases
In the Great Chamber
You don't have to drink ambrosia-tinted elixirs
Or scream about the absolute frailty of a god
Who condones perpetuities of suffering
You don't have to believe in wooden crucifixes
Or clay figurines in pastel-veneer beads
Or cranberry-glass words you can seal the Aeolian-
Gossamer tendrils of your saffron-diapason soul
In tarantella-white constellations of asphodel-pulsing,
Lily-chanting twilight.

Of Amaranth-Prophetic Mirrors

Emerald-sealing amphoras of Nostell-gentian light
Transform the dust of time to gladiolus-dreaming, corolla-
 effulgent
Galleries of orange-pilastered, hydrangea-vaned timelessness
To Albano-red amplitudes of autumn-musing, dusk-
Germinating light as a Dresden-spectral daemon
Shapes amber-liminal, Buttermere-permeating harmonies
Of sunset-enchanted wisdom in Thames-fusing, rainbow-
Sentient angles of amaranth-prophetic, jasmine-breathing
Mirrors.

OF MAGENTA-VERNAL HIEROGLYPHS

An oaken-gabled line of pilaster-terraced white
Where the oleander-misting sea meets the dahlia-
Curving shore in a lilac-molding ecstasy of triadic-
Urned deluges a rosewood-tapering pastiche of madrigal-
Shearing fountains filters adamanthine-glowing sunrises
Through the portico-yellow ruins of a Tivoli-ancient
Graveyard Iliad-pale names whitewashed by candelabra-
Splintering silences saving the dead from the draconian
Vicissitudes of hourglass-sated rituals a crystal-trimmed
Sacristy of magenta-vernal hieroglyphs preserves the bronze-
Winding castle of the soul a Veronese-refulgent fresco
Of fleur-de-lys-concealing seeds of Polyhymnia delight
Shapes oriel-crossing masks of Caen-sutured heavens
As campanile-turquoise stained-glass pink-lunettes
Blow gently across sacred-opalescent, Ionic-looming glades.

Creating the Hyacinth-Streaming Twilight

In the jasmine-templed aura of the Lytes Cary-majestic
Pines the elves create the hyacinth-streaming twilight
In delphinium-glistening breaths of Aeolian-lyred
   longing

The iris-blossoming evening wind fills
The meadows, sea, and forests with sibylline-
Cairned melodies of Chopin-mystical solitudes
Shaping reflections of bronze-prismed timelessness
In amber-scented intimations of forsythia-pealing,
   red-opalescent horizons

In the poppy-effulgent phantasm of the damask-
Gloaming cypress-aureoles I listen
To ancient-prophetic curves and lavender-
Angled tears of sunset-lingering
   sarabandes

In the asphodel-iridescent silences
Of the sacred grove the elves shape
Twilight cascades of maroon-stamened
Eternity in the velvet-chasmed infinitudes
Of my jade-astered soul in the Chartres-
Veined light of a thousand dove-sceptered
Mirrors I reshape my saffron-breathing soul
In crystalline-gelatinous murmurings
   of Turner-melodic light.

I Am a Goldau-Misting Tapestry

I am a Goldau-misting tapestry
Of unicorn-dreaming, Elysian-tendrilled snow-aureoles
Shaping the first day of spring in cypress-radiant
Cantatas of pearl-shadowed, onyx-soaring synergies
Sealing the flux of time in phoenix-dewed silences
Of Harlaxton-exulting, velvet-trembling light
I am the hyacinth-weaving, amaranth-diapason heart
Of the Gobelin-streaming, Pythian-veined wind
Carving apocalyptic-jade blossoms of magenta-perfecting
Genesis on amaryllis-chiming, marble-gloaming mirrors.

The Ghost at Kenilworth

In the gray-spindling evening the ghost at Kenilworth
Walks through the tiara-plumed, oleander-corniced portal
And the Gemini-astered priory-gate into the jade-apsed
Mists of the heliotrope-conceiving, Byzantine-furrowed
Cemetery where every grave awaits his gentle-mitred,
Hieratic-gleaming caresses where every grave knows
That he will bathe magenta-liminal helixes in the yellow-
Amaranth light of his nepenthe-linden soul
Where every spirit, recently buried or centuries old,
Feels the semblance of eternity in the cumulus-graceful
Magnanimity of his dynastic-martyred presence
The ghost at Kenilworth shares damask-pinioned globes
Of Aeolian-effusive light with diastolic-amber souls
Rising from wine-stamened, cypress-germinating pallors.

In Emerald-Veiled Panoplies

A Mansart-effulgent castle of tabernacle-gray, ivy-wreathed
Silences emerges where Zarathustra-liminal lives rest
Like mosaic-pristine leaves on frost-tipped, pointillist-
Glistening marsh-staves, a pergola-seething, baroque-ringing
Castle where Tudor-inflecting, parapet-listening souls live
Forever in Lido-breathless stillnesses, a Jacobean-panelled,
Grail-enchanting castle where the nabi-intimate, dawn-eglantine
Promises of talisman-projecting, amaranth-prophetic tapestries
Are fulfilled in emerald-veiled, diastolic-yearning panoplies
Of hermetic-altared, Matisse-crystalline light conceiving
An auburn-vaulting singing-tree in the Marburg-sacred
Courtyard beyond the ruby-ephemeral smiles shaping saffron-
Architraved melodies of Montacute-streaming timelessness
In velvet-spinning murmurs of twilight-extending, asphodel-
Blossoming eyes.

A Solitary Figure

An Aeolian-solitary figure listening to the primordial
Concurrence of the evening waves, watching the crystalline-
Panelling horizon shape mosaic-sapphire tonal-mists
Into hieratic-white epochs of grail-resplendent amplitudes
And megalithic-yellow Kandinsky-silences,

A Delphic-solitary figure along mangrove-jade interludes
Of heron-magenta light and kithara-nesting seagull-
Destinies walking into dune-astered, Blickling-pure
Thresholds of anemone-irrigating, auburn-rhapsodic light,

A mauve-saturated unity of intense-springing metamorphoses
Along the dusk-anvilled shore listening to the Rhine-sublime
Presence of bronze-gloaming, damask-nocturne solitudes
And the aureole-whispering, Rembrandt-amaryllis chimes of
    eternity.

I Am an Amber-Prophetic Stone

I am a madonna-wise piece of andante-liminal stone
Creating Gothic-torrential, Marmorsaal-radiant manor-
Aureoles consecrating silver-encircling silences
Of hyacinth-spiritual shadows in stained-glass triptychs
Of phoenix-empyrean mazes waiting for the melisma-
Spinning evening sun to touch zodiac-destined, wisteria-
Grottoed leaves around me in a crimson-apsed ferment
Of Neuschwanstein-soaring solitudes

I am an amber-prophetic stone speaking in the dusk-
Gloaming tones of porcelain-twilight, sunflower-yearning
Paradise I am the Turner-eloquent soul of the jonquil-
Glorifying chandelier encompassing the sacred-
Illuminating profundity of the ancient-timbered,
Dynastic-proportioned aura in universe-spanning
Thresholds of Petworth-magnanimous, amaranth-
Effulgent space

I am an Amsterdam-vaned stone washed by nocturne-soft
Horizons sealing the reveries of the lotus-shaping moat
In crescent-dewed silhouettes of astral-corniced time
I am a diadem-templed stone breathing Elysian-tendrilled
Intimations of heliotrope-swirling light over the deluge-
Flickering fields and mandolin-cairned meadows
I am a Delft-pealing stone weaving the acropolis-saving
Silences of the asphodel-helixed wind in pomegranate-
Leavening mirrors of Ruisdael-lambent, acanthus-golden light.